LORD,
DO YOU HEAR ME?

Edited by

SISTER MAUREEN SKELLY, SCH

M𝔹

The Regina Press
New York

1986
THE REGINA PRESS
145 Sherwood Avenue
Farmingdale, N.Y. 11735

The Regina Press would like to thank the children from Mt. Manresa Retreat House on Staten Island, N.Y., whose prayers and hard work made this book possible.

Cover design: Jeff Thurau, Roth Advertising
Cover photography: Chris Sheridan

ISBN: 0-88271-134-2

Printed in Belgium

CONTENTS

INTRODUCTION 5

GOD 6

FAMILY 18

THE WORLD 46

FRIENDS 64

MYSELF 72

*I would like to dedicate
this book to my parents,
who taught me how to pray.*

INTRODUCTION

The world today is quite complex and has many problems. These problems, especially when seen through the eyes of today's youth, can appear to be overwhelming. In searching for answers to these problems, people of all ages turn to God.

LORD, DO YOU HEAR ME? presents a collection of prayers written by the youth of today for the youth of today. This is what makes this book unique. Situations and problems ranging from family to super power relations are covered within these pages. What better way to explore the relationship between today's youth and God than to have the young people themselves actually relate their innermost feelings toward God and the world around them.

The prayers that follow were contributed by boys and girls, ages 9-14, while they were retreatants at Mount Manresa Retreat House in Staten Island, New York. May their prayers help you strengthen your relationship with God and those around you.

Sister Maureen Skelly

GOD

THANK YOU FOR A LOVELY GIFT

Lord, thank you for your lovely gift and the scenery on top of the mountain.
I really loved it. It was nice and sunny and there was lots of fresh green grass.
I never knew it could be so green and beautiful and never thought there could be so much of it. The sky was beautiful and clear. I loved everything. Thank you again. Amen.

PRAYER OF THANKSGIVING

Lord, thank you for all the good things you have given me. When you touch my heart, it feels like pieces coming together. When you touch my eyes it feels like a twinkle. When you touch my ears they feel like I can hear anything. Thank you for being with me. Amen.

THE GIFT OF LIFE

God, it is good to be alive and I thank you dearly. My life on your earth is most precious to me and to my loved ones. While I am here, I am trying to experience all that I can and to live my life in peace like you have. Lord, I love this world and everything you have created. I know when you call me, my life on earth will have been fulfilled and that it is time to start my life over again with you in heaven! Amen.

✠

PRAYER OF THANKS

Thank you for your love; my family; and friends.
For the love of God never ends.
Thank you for the clothes we wear,
And everything that we share. Amen.

THANK YOU, GOD

We thank you, God, for our lives and the food and the drink you have given us. We feel your power when we pray for forgiveness. We pray for peace, love and unity in the world. We also ask for your help when something goes wrong. Amen.

HELP ME BELIEVE MORE

Lord, please strengthen my faith, my love and my hope in you. I feel I am slipping from the Church and from you. I need to reassure myself of your love and your presence. It saddens me that I have these feelings but I know you will help. Amen.

PRAYER OF A HAPPY PERSON

God, when I wake up in the morning it feels so good to be alive. When I go to bed at night, I thank you that I survived the day. I think of all the people who have died during just one day and I realize how good it is to be alive. Amen.

PRAYER OF HELP FOR SCHOOL

Thank you, Lord, for giving me that extra push whenever I need it. I feel like quitting but you help me to keep my head up and press on through the trials of school life. Please, grant me the grace to fight off the pressures of high school. I know I will be pushed to my limits and will need all the help I can get. Thank you, God. Amen.

WHEN GOD IS OUR FRIEND

It's good to be alive even though we doubt life itself sometimes. God, are you my friend? I'd like to know. I need someone now; someone to hold. You are so special to me. When I'm sad you make me smile. Won't you spend some time with me to dream? Just for a little while?
It's good to be alive. It's certainly true...because I am most happy when I'm spending time with you. Amen.

THANK GOD FOR BIRDS!

Dear God, thank you for the effort you put in making our world even more beautiful by giving us birds. They give us sweet music and delight us with their exotic feathers. Amen.

PRAYER IN APPRECIATION OF NATURE

God, you made the pebbles that we skip in the pond and the clouds in the sky that are always changing. You made the breeze that cools us and the sun that warms us. Your sense of humor is shown by the duck-billed platypus I saw. Sometimes, I don't even stop long enough to look at the flowers. So, God, for all your creation; Thanks! Amen.

PRAYER OF APPRECIATION

Thank you, God, for all the things that make our lives beautiful. We thank you for the rain and the sun that make our lovely flowers grow. We thank you for the rain that gives us water to quench our thirst. We thank you for the sun that warms our lives. God, we love you and all the beautiful gifts you have given us. Amen.

THANK GOD FOR HUMOR!

Thank you, God, for the humorous
things that help me smile even when
I am depressed. Thank you for ostriches
to laugh at; monkeys and donkeys,
elephants and rhinos, too. They brighten
my days. Most of all thank you for me.
Amen.

PRAYER OF THANKSGIVING

Thank you, God, for funny things
For hippos, monkeys and other things,
For bees that sting and bells that ring,
Thank you, God, for everything! Amen.

THANK YOU, GOD!

Thank you, God, for the things that fly.
Thank you, God, for the things up high.
Thank you, God, for all in the sky.
Thank you, God, for bees that sting.
Thank you, God, for living things.
Amen.

A THOUGHTFUL PRAYER

Birds are graceful, they can fly.
Birds don't sin, I don't know why.
Birds are like God in a way.
I think it's through the birds I'll pray.
Amen.

A SIMPLE PRAYER

Please, God, I pray for those who do not appreciate the simplest things like the rain, the snow or the sun, because the simplest things are the most beautiful. Amen.

PRAYER TO JESUS

Dear God, help the people of our Parish be more like Jesus. May we forgive others as Jesus did. May we love others as Jesus loves us. May those who are going to receive Confirmation fulfill their promises as good forgiving Christians. Amen.

PRAYER WHEN THINGS GO WRONG

Dear God, we pray when things go wrong. Help us to be patient and help us to work things out. We know that if we trust you, you will help us in our time of need. Amen.

THE PRAYER OF ONE WHO IS GRATEFUL

Lord, thank you for your wonderful gift. It meant so much to me. When you came to my home everything lit up...even me. It was pleasing to see you. I felt all the broken pieces in my heart come back together and I love people ten times more than I loved them before. Jesus, I love you and you are special to me in every way. Amen.

PRAYER OF ONE WHO LOVES CREATION

God, you have put me in charge of the earth. You have given me the responsibility to take care of your creation and to love it. You have helped me through the good times and the bad times. For that, thank you. I thank you for putting me in charge of the glorious things you made. I ask that you help me always. I love you God. Amen.

FAMILY

PRAYER TO MY PARENTS

God, I thank my parents for so many things which have helped me a lot; for giving birth to me and for being around to care. They take me to places and give me food and clothing. But most of all, I love them a lot because of their love and affection for me. Amen.

PRAYER FOR PARENTS

God bless the parents of today.
Help them be strong and in control.
Guide them in making wise decisions.
May they live a holy life.
May they always be faithful to God.
May they be faithful to each other and
    their families.
May they carry out their responsibilities
    with love and patience. Amen.

PRAYER OF A CHILD WHEN BOTH PARENTS HAVE DIED

Dear God, will you help me with my new life? My parents died and I am all alone. Please help me find new parents fast. When you find new parents please make them love and care for me the way my old parents cared for me. When my parents died, it was like I died and the inside of me fell apart. So, God, please bless me and help me to love and care for my new parents. At the same time, help me not to forget my old parents. Amen.

PRAYER OF THANKSGIVING

Dear God, thank you for blessing our family. When you touched my heart I felt the power of love, freedom and understanding of peace. Once again, thanks for caring about me and my family. Amen.

FOR STRENGTH TO BEAR A CROSS

Bless me, Father, for I am scared. Give me the strength to be loving and patient and the sister I should be. My brother was born retarded and I feel helpless. I want to hold him and try to make him understand, but I know it will not do any good. When I tell him I love him I know he doesn't understand, but I feel in my heart and soul that somehow he does understand. Amen.

WHEN MY PARENTS ARGUE

I get scared and want to go away, Lord, far away from them. I wish my parents wouldn't fight. So that's why I pray to you, Lord. Help them to stop so that I won't be afraid. Please Lord, I don't want to go far away. Amen.

WHEN MY PARENTS ARGUE

Dear God, when my parents argue, it seems as if the world is erupting. The loud voices of their screaming and yelling seem to tear my eardrums out. Their insults hurt me more than they hurt themselves. I don't have any respect for either one of them because when they hurt each other they hurt me. Please help them to try and understand each other. Help them to try and deal with their problems in a mature manner. I love my parents and I don't want to see them hurt our family. Amen.

✝

PRAYER FOR ARGUING PARENTS

As the night creeps in, I can only hear the hollow sound of the wind echoing outside my window. ''Is that you, God?'' I'm so alone. I need you, Lord. The tears stream down my cheeks with no one there to wipe them dry. When two people you love so dearly tear at each other's heart, a part of you seems to die. Lord, every night the shouts grow louder than ever...My heart has grown cold. I sit here alone and curse them for forgetting that the love they once shared for one another was found through you and through this love I came to be. Lord, take my hand, help me grow strong. Keep me warm with your love. I know you are there for me. Amen.

FOR UNDERSTANDING PARENTS

Dear God, I understand that my parents care for me and love me, but I want them to understand me and my needs as well as their own. I love my parents. I know they love me. Help me to understand why they do what they do. Help us see the light of Jesus and to be friends as well as family. God, I love you and I know my parents do too. Help us and take care of us. We want to be with you now and forever on earth and in heaven. Amen.

PRAYER FOR WHEN PARENTS ARGUE

Dear Lord, when my parents argue I feel helpless and confused. I know that they are hurting each other and there is nothing I can do. Please help me. I close my eyes and cover my ears and wish my problems would disappear. But when I open my eyes they are still there before me. Give me strength and give them the grace to love one another. Amen.

FOR A JOB

Dear God, I am calling on you now in my hour of need. A person whom I love is going through too much. He just lost his job and lost all his hope. Help him find the way back to a better life than before. Amen.

LIFE IN THE FAST LANE

Lord, our brother is only 16 and has already discovered the bad side of life. Unfortunately, he chose to follow it. We hate to see such a good person get hooked on drugs. We get scared when we think of what could happen if he overdoses. Please God, guide him through this terrible turn of life. Help him to see the light of goodness and make the right decision. We love him very much and care a lot. Amen.

FOR PARENTS

Thank you, God, for parents—
For their support, guidance and love.
Their love for us is as strong
As God's love up above. Amen.

FOR A PERSON OUT OF WORK

Dear God, please help my family. We are trying but it is so hard sometimes. We try not to ask for anything but we need food. My Mother is always crying because we don't have money for the things we need. My Father either sits quietly or yells because he is so upset about not working. Everything is falling apart. We are trying hard and we are putting all our faith in you. Amen.

PRAYER OF ONE WHOSE PARENTS HAVE DIED

O, God, I feel so hurt inside. Please help me, God, through this terrible time. O, Dear God, please assist me through this time. Amen.

PRAYER FOR A HANDICAPPED BROTHER

Dear God, please help my brother to be strong and resist feeling bad when other kids ridicule him for his handicap. Also, Lord, would you please help me be strong for him? He needs all the strength he can get. I also need your help to enable my brother to do for himself and to be able to take care of himself. He is a human being just like everyone else and should be treated with dignity and respect. He just needs a chance. Amen.

+

PRAYER FOR A RETARDED SISTER

Dear God, I just want to say a few words to you. I really need your help. My sister is retarded. I love her a lot, and wish it were me instead of her. Please help me cope with this. I don't know what to do. Please help me accept this. I want her to get well. She is only ten years old and I'd like her to experience life to the fullest as I have. Thanks, God. Amen.

✝

FOR STRENGTH TO CARRY ON

Dear Lord, please give me strength to carry on in these trying times. Although I am bereft of one of my parents, I need to go on. I have a life to live. Help me not to be negligent of my Catholic beliefs and life. I sincerely need your help. Amen.

PRAYER TO USE THE FAMILY CAR

Dear God, I know it's been a long time but I'd really like to talk to you. God, help me to be trustworthy of my parents. One thing I would like more than anything is to borrow my father's car. Please help my father understand that I am a responsible person and that I will be most careful. I know this may be asking a lot but will you at least think about it. Please take into consideration how much it would mean to me not only to borrow the car but to know that my parents trust me? Thank you. Amen.

✚

FOR MY BROTHER

Dear God, why must my brother's life be this way? I thank you every day that I am strong and healthy, but it breaks my heart to see my brother live his life this way. Please God, help this child to be happy and successful in the world. Please lighten his other burdens and help him through. Be with him because he needs you. He is very special and I love him. Give him a goal in life and help him reach his goal. Make people love him and understand him. Dear God, don't let his life be miserable and useless. Amen.

✝

OUT OF WORK

Dear God, right now we need your help. Dad is out of work and cannot provide my family with what we need. Everyday he goes out and looks for a job but people do not need help. All he does is fight with everyone in our house. I feel very bad. God, please point me in the right direction so I can find a job and provide my family with what they need. Amen.

PRAYER WHEN YOU HAVE AN UNEMPLOYED PARENT

Dear God, I know it can be hard for people to find a good job, but why does my Dad have to be unemployed? He has responsibilities, a wife and 2 children to support. God, it is so hard to see my Dad upset. Please help him find a job. Amen.

HELP TO OVERCOME DEPRESSION

Dear God, help me and my family to overcome the depression that we are suffering. Give my father the strength to keep the faith that he will find a job. Help us through these hard times and to remember that you are with us through it all. Thank you. Amen.

WHEN FINANCES ARE LOW

Dear God, help my family cope with our financial situation and not to lose hope in each other. We need you to give us strength and to be our inspiration. Help me not to let the things that other kids say bother me. As long as I know that you love me, I can be confident in myself. Thank you. Amen.

PRAYER FOR A DISABLED SISTER

Lord, please help my sister, the child whom you chose to be different. All of us who love her cannot understand why she was chosen by you. Please understand that we cannot stand to see her suffer. It hurts us so much. Lord, please make her better and give all of us the serenity to accept her. Most importantly, help her to accept herself. Amen.

✝

UNEMPLOYMENT

Dear God, my father is out of work. We have barely enough money to support a family of six. Why does this always have to happen to hardworking and willing people like my father? I don't understand. While criminals are getting away with stealing, good people are suffering. Please help! Amen.

PRAYER OF THE CHILD OF ARGUING PARENTS

Lord, when my parents argue, I get the feeling inside me that I am not wanted. I feel that it always falls back on me. Dear Lord, help me get over this feeling. I know it's not my fault that they are fighting. I love them very much. Please bless them and let them love one another. O, God, please hear my prayer and bring my family back together again. Amen.

PRAYER FOR A BIRTHDAY PARTY

Dear God, my birthday is next week. Please put it into my Mom's mind to give me a party. I have tried to be a good person and to do things with a smile. I am happy to be alive, too. So, let's have a celebration! Amen.

PRAYER FOR A DISABLED SISTER

Lord, help my sister. I try to do all I can for her, but sometimes it's not enough. It breaks my heart to see her not being able to do all the wonderful things I can do; to experience life. It's really not fair. If it is your will that she be this way, please shine some grace on her. Lend her a helping hand because, Lord, I love her. Amen.

✝

SINGLE PARENT PRAYER

Dear God, please show my mother how much I really love her. Please make other people understand that she is special. She shows more love than any person I know. Another mother might not put up with the hard times that she does. She is not only my mother, but also my father. Amen.

A PRAYER OF THANKS FOR GOD'S LOVE

Thank you for coming and lighting up the hearts of my family. You brought peace and love into our hearts and lives. When you touched my heart all the anger and pain disappeared and the broken pieces came back together. You shed the light of life, love, peace and kindness into my family and me. I thank you, Jesus, with all my heart. Amen.

PRAYER TO OVERCOME JEALOUSY

Help me, dear God, to overcome the jealousy I feel over my little brother.
I want to thank you for giving us a little baby, even though it hurts when my parents ignore me when he's around.
Give me faith and strength so that I can grow with my brother instead of being angry with him. Thank you. Amen.

PRAYER FOR MY BROTHER

Lord, my brother wants to use the car and my parents keep saying, ''No.''
God, I don't want to pray for the wrong thing, but I would like them to trust him.
He is careful. God, you know best. Help them both do what is right. Amen.

DEATH OF A BROTHER

Dear God, I ask you to help me through this crisis in my life. Please forgive me if I don't understand, but my brother's death is hard to accept. Why did he have to die so young? It does not seem fair. God, How can you let something like this happen? He was the only real friend I had. Please help me. Amen.

IT'S NOT MY TURN!

I know it's not my turn God, but I won't complain because you never did. I know it seems unfair, but that is the way life is sometimes. I know these chores seem so little compared to carrying a cross. Even though it's not my turn, I'll do it anyway. Amen.

PRAYER FOR PARENTS

Lord, help my parents with any spiritual problems they might have. Give them the wisdom to make the right decisions about family, friends and other concerns. Help them to understand and relate to their children, so that their relationship will be stronger. Help them to keep their faith in God so that they can face the difficulties of life. Please watch over and take care of them. Amen.

✝

PRAYER OF ONE WHO HAS HAD A MISUNDERSTANDING WITH PARENTS

Dear Father, please forgive me for all the trouble I have put my parents through. Please help me to ask for forgiveness for the things I have done wrong. I love my parents and am sorry I have caused them worry. Amen.

PRAYER FOR A MARRIED SISTER/BROTHER

Dear God, please watch over my brother/sister in their life with their new companion. May their lives be filled with joy and happiness. Bring them through hardships and suffering. Guide them through the night so they may wake up to a better tomorrow. If they fall away bring them back to your Church and your love. May there always be peace and love in their home. Look over them wherever they go, and let them succeed in all they do. Amen.

✝

PRAYER FOR ALCOHOLIC PARENTS

Lord, I am your child. I am feeling alone in this distressful home of alcoholics. I am afraid it will never grow peaceful. I need your love, warmth and understanding. Guide me, Lord. Amen.

✟

God, help my parents see that they don't need liquor. They have me, their child, who loves them very much. I don't even know if they love me or if they know how much they hurt me. I need your love, God, to help me through this time in my life. Amen.

WHEN MY PARENTS ARGUE

Dear Father, I do understand that people have disagreements, but why are there so many? Why do they last for such a long period of time? I know my parents love me very much and I love them just the same, but sometimes I feel I am the cause of it all. God, please help me live through this and help my parents to try and understand each other better. If I am the cause please help me to understand the reason why. Amen.

PRAYER FOR UNDERSTANDING

Hi, God, it's me again. Listen, I wish my mother could be more understanding sometimes...All my friends are going to the movies Friday night and she thinks that I should be in the house with my family. At 13 years old, come on! These years are supposed to be fun and Mom is so overprotective. I know she loves me and worries about me, but she doesn't realize that her little girl is growing into a young woman. I guess I should really try and talk to her. Maybe she will listen and maybe she won't. Even if it doesn't change anything she will at least know how I feel. Well, thanks for listening. Amen.

✝

PRAYER TO USE THE FAMILY CAR

Dear God, I know it is not easy to be a parent. I guess I won't know what it's like until I become one myself. Please help me to understand them and let them understand me. They love me and are afraid to give me the car. They feel I might get hurt. If they would only give me a chance to be myself and be independent they would know I can handle it. Please let my parents trust me with the car and help me to be understanding and trustworthy. Amen.

+

THE WORLD

PRAYER FOR SPACE TRAVELERS

Dear Lord, you made the universe in seven days. We are curious, Lord, about what else you created and we want to explore space. We want to seek what is beyond the frontier. Please God, give us the ability and the knowledge to make everything as safe as possible for the journey of future astronauts. Amen.

PRAYER FOR ASTRONAUTS

Dear Father, we talk often. When we do I ask for your help. We must discover and in discovering we must learn. Protect us. Protect our astronauts who are the instruments of our learning. Protect their children and their families who let them go to further our cause. Protect our children who are the future of our world. Amen.

PRAYER FOR THE HOMELESS

God, Father Almighty, grant that homeless people do not suffer from the cold and harsh weather. Help us to give them shelter and food so that they will not die of disease and hunger. By the power of Christ may these people receive what they need when they need it. Amen.

PRAYER FOR NO NUCLEAR WAR

Dear God, give the people of Russia and the United States courage. Try and help them disarm nuclear weapons. Help our countries settle their differences peacefully. May world peace come soon. Please God, let us live our life without war. Amen.

PRAYER FOR SPECIAL CHILDREN—THE CRIPPLED

Dear God, sometimes I get all wrapped up in my own problems and forget about those who have larger problems than mine. As a normal and healthy child I do not know the pain and suffering special children and crippled children experience. Help me to always remember and pray for these children in my daily prayers. God, you must love them so much, but why do they have to go through life like that? What did they do to deserve it? Is it their fault? Thanks God. Amen.

+

PRAYER FOR VOCATIONS

Dear God, we need you to bring us more priests and nuns. Open up the hearts of people who really want to help people. In this way, these people will help us understand God even more. Thank you, God. Keep us in your prayers. Amen.

PRAYER FOR PEACE

God, inspire us to be peace makers. Let us bring peace to all your people. May we help those who are in trouble. Let me bring peace to those who are fighting or arguing with each other. Amen.

PRAYER FOR THE HOMELESS

Dear Father, I thank you for giving me life and giving me wonderful parents. I have a big problem. Last week I went on a trip with my friend and his wonderful family. On this trip I saw a poor little boy who looked very hungry and I didn't have any food for him. He looked like an orphan. Please, God, help me help this poor boy and others like him. Amen.

PRAYER FOR NEWCOMERS

Dear God, I pray for all the children who face a new life in a different environment. Please help them on their new quest. Help them to fit in. Make them feel like a small fish in a big comfortable pond. Amen.

PRAYER FOR HELP FOR THE WORLD

The world is so messed up, God.
That much you know.
With all your children dying,
How can we make it grow?
All the things we do wrong,
You show how much you care,
Then why do we despair?
God, you can help us,
Turn the world around
Make us whole again and heaven bound.
God, can you change this world, too?
If we do our part,
Your help will see us through. Amen.

THE WORLD IS SO MESSED UP, LORD

The world is so messed up, Lord. There is war, hunger, poverty, sickness and death. Everywhere I turn I see one of these problems and always wish you would have some mercy and give us a reprieve. Make the world a little better, give us a start to make the world a better place. We have come a long way from the cavemen but we still have a long way to go. This prayer is from one person who really cares what happens to the people whom you created from the likeness of yourself. People are dying because of these problems and there are many more who care; but we can't do it on our own. We need help from you. Why is the world so messed up? Help us Lord. Please! Amen.

PRAYER FOR HOMELESS PEOPLE

We pray to you, O Lord, for all the homeless people in the world that we live in today. We pray that our communities will participate in keeping love alive and in helping homeless people find shelter. Amen.

PRAYER FOR PEACE

Dear Lord, I pray that peace may be widely practiced in the future; that our country, and other countries stop producing deadly arms to blow each other up. May these countries use the money originally planned for weapons to feed, clothe and shelter a hungry world. Amen.

PRAYER FOR THE WORLD

Dearest Father of all in heaven and earth, give us strength! Give us the strength to resist the wrongs of this present world: poverty, abortion, drugs, murder and war. All of these are mankind's destruction against itself. It soon will be a lifeless world. Help us to eliminate this disease of destruction that is an epidemic. All of us have a part of you in our hearts. It is that part of us that will overcome life's setbacks. Amen.

FOR WORLD LEADERS

Dear Father, please help our President come to peace with all the world leaders so we do not have to live in fear of nuclear war. Help them realize how much damage and danger nuclear war can put us in. Amen.

PRAYER FOR THE WORLD

Lord, in this world you have created, there are many good things but also many bad things. Help the homeless men, women, and children who unfortunately live in streets and abandoned houses. Lord, please help them so that they may seek and find a peaceful place to live in comfort. Lord, if possible show and give me the ability to help them get where they should be, in an atmosphere of love and togetherness. Amen.

✛

PRAYER FOR A SHY PERSON

Live a little, enjoy life... take time to have fun. God gave you life to use and live, to grow in yourself and with others. Go out and give yourself to the world and make the world yours... the city, the country... No force, no pressure... Solitude and community. Love. Amen.

FOR THOSE IN NEED

Lord, I know I have many things in my life: a home, family, friends. I also know of the thousands upon thousands of people who don't have any of that; not by their own fault but because of the courses their lives have taken. All I ask is for you to give them much of your love and much of your time because they need it all. Even if you want, take some of what's mine and share it among them. Because Lord, love begins and grows in a home. Amen.

HELP OF GOD FOR THE PEOPLE OF THE WORLD

Dear Father, please help all the people on earth who are dying in wars or by starvation. We need your help to end all wars and to live in peace. We also need your help to allow us to share our things so that we all have our equal share. Thank you, Father. Amen.

I WISH THINGS WERE BETTER

Dear God, I wish things were better in the world. There is too much hate where there should be love. Where there is love there is too little of it. God, help us to appreciate all the things we have and not to wish for bigger and better things. Teach us to be satisfied and happy with our lives. When we are happy, let us think of others who are less fortunate. Amen.

✙

PRAYER FOR ACCEPTANCE OF ALL PEOPLES

Lord, help me understand why people don't like to meet different types of people. I, myself, came from Italy not knowing how to speak English. Everyone laughed at me. I tried to laugh with them but after a while it began to hurt. Please, Lord, help me to understand. Amen.

PRAYER FOR ALL SPECIAL PEOPLE IN THE WORLD

Lord, help all the special people in the world, all those who have a handicap and can't always help themselves. Give them the special attention and love they so rightly deserve. Make them feel they can do anything they want. With your help and guidance I know they can. Most of all give me the strength and courage to help these people help themselves. I know they need my love and I want to share it with them. Amen.

PRAYER FOR A SICK PERSON

Be not afraid. The Lord will be with you always. The Lord will help you. Amen.

PRAYER FOR SPACE TRAVELERS

Dear Lord, help those who wander to another place, who have the adventurous spirit to go beyond this planet we live on; the people who have the courage to explore another frontier. Give them a sense of pride, strength and protection. For those who have accepted that challenge and have gone beyond the frontier, bless them because they have given their lives for what they believed in. They are now in a place beyond this planet! Bless them. Amen.

✝

PRAYER FOR THE WORLD

The world is so messed up, God, I just
can't believe the things that are going on
today. We have people fighting in wars,
and people trying to kill each other;
drugs, abortion, poverty and so many
other things. I wish, dear Lord, you
would do something to stop all this
because sometimes it really scares me.
With all the talk of nuclear war I am
afraid sometimes that I might not wake
up the next morning. Dear Lord, please
try to relieve all the problems in the
world today and bring peace and
harmony throughout the universe.
Amen.

PRAYER FOR A MIXED UP WORLD

God, I live my life day by day hoping that it will get better. All the pain and suffering in the world has filled my heart with sorrow. I look forward to the day when we will all live as one and forgive each other's sins and be a family once again. Oh Lord, please answer my prayer when I ask you to help us. The world is so messed up, God. Amen.

FOR THE HOMELESS

Dear God, please provide the homeless with the care they need. Give them the strength to live their lives and not give up what little they have. Let them live their lives to the fullest. Let them know you love them and will always be with them no matter what the consequences are. Amen.

FOR THE WORLD AND FOR THOSE WHO DIE FOR PEACE

Dear God, please help out with the success of world peace and the people who must put their lives in danger for this peace. Help the ties of the world to become stronger so we can learn and experiment together. May we learn faster and help solve our problems more quickly. Take care of the people who have lost their lives doing this and the people who will lose their lives in time to come. Amen.

✝

FRIENDS

IN THANKSGIVING FOR A FRIEND

Thank you, O Lord, for one of my most precious gifts, my friend. A friend is a special gift who will be with me always and show me how much she cares each day. It is a permanent symbol of love that will always stay in my heart. Each day I am reminded of how special she is. Amen.

PRAYER OF A NEW STUDENT

Dear God, I'm a new student from out of town.
Please help me make friends and get around. Amen.

FOR RECONCILIATION WITH A FRIEND

Dear God, in my life I have hurt many people: my family and my friends. One that I have hurt the most is my friend. She has stuck by me through thick and thin. When I felt I needed more companionship, I left her for another popular group of people. In the end when they had enough of me I went crawling back to her and she rejected me. God, please help her to see I am sorry for leaving her and I want us to be as close as we were before. Amen.

+

MY FRIEND HAS MOVED AWAY

My friend moved away and I am all alone. I have nobody to cheer me up when I am feeling down. Nobody to express all my feelings to. I never even had a chance to tell that person I was there for them. Please, God, help me. I know if you do, I can make it through this terrible crisis, because, God, you are my friend. Amen.

THEY CALL ME NAMES

Lord, for the times I have been ridiculed, give me guidance and help me. Names hurt more than bruises because bruises go away. I know they called you names but that does not take away my hurt and pain. Keep me in your heart for I know your name for me. You call me, ''Friend.'' Help me, God, my friend. Amen.

THE PRAYER OF ONE BETRAYED BY A FRIEND

Please God, put a closing feeling and an
    end,
To a friendship that no one can mend.
I can't believe what I've been through
This feeling is so new.
She looked and gave me an expressionless
    face,
Making me wonder and feel out of place.
Oh, God, help the tears stop and my
    feelings heal.
Without my friend, life seems so far away.
This feeling is common and Lord, it
    won't go away.
You might know, Lord, the feeling:
    BETRAY. Amen.

PRAYER FOR ACCEPTANCE

Dear God, You know how it feels to be rejected or left out by your friends. I feel like this all the time. I feel like I'm different from my friends and they don't want to be bothered with me. If I had one wish, I wish that my friends would be closer to me and make me one of the crowd. Everyone needs friends and without them I will not have happiness. Amen.

✝

PRAYER OF ONE WHO IS TRYING

God, help me to accept who I am and what I do. Sometimes I do things just to become popular with my friends. Sometimes I strike out at you, God, but you always call me to bat again. Help me, God, to be a good player on your team. Amen.

PRAYER OF ONE ALL ALONE

God, my friend has left me; my sympathizer, my helper, the one who goes everywhere and does everything I do. My follower and guide, my loved enemy, the one I care for most, and the one who gets on my nerves most. You are gone. Part of me is gone. Who can replace you?

God, can you be my friend? I'm not sure of you. You seem so far away, so distant. I cannot seem to reach you except in the depths of my mind. Come closer to me. God, let me come closer to you. Almost...almost, I can just about touch you. I can nearly feel you, I can almost trust you. I know you will always be there, God, waiting to be my friend. I want to be yours. Amen.

✝

PRAYER OF A NEW KID IN TOWN

O my God, bless me and help me to make new friends. I am a new kid on the block and I'd like to fit in with everyone else. It's hard when you are a new kid in town because everyone picks on you. The other kids think I'm different and they don't want to take me as their friend. I need your help now more than ever. Please help to make things easier for me. Amen.

PEER PRESSURE

Lord, I feel I have been rejected by my friends. They don't understand how I feel when they pressure me into things I feel are wrong. Please give me the courage that I need to stand up to them because they will pick on me if I'm different. Please make them understand. Amen.

MYSELF

ON BEING FREE

At one time I was chained down.
I have discovered new life, I am free.
At one time I was suffering.
I have discovered new hope, I am free.
Long ago there was nothing left for me.
I have discovered new love, I am free.
My newly gained freedom has my spirit
    roaming free.
My dreams are soaring, my life
    enriched. Amen.

✙

PRAYER OF A WINNER

Dear Heavenly Father, when we win a
game, help us to be good sportsmen.
Grant that we will not tease other people
because they lost. Help us so we will not
think we are the best, but that we used
the talents you gave us to the fullest.
Amen.

PRAYER FOR THOSE ON DRUGS

Dear Lord, I pray that you help those who choose to destroy their lives with drugs and alcohol. These people do not have anyone to turn to so they live a life of unhappiness. Please Lord, show them the way to turn away from things that will hurt them and take them away from you. Help them and send them a friend who can guide them. Amen.

✚

THEY CALL ME, "MR. EXCUSES"

Dear Lord, I am sorry for the times I have made excuses or put the blame on someone else, and for the misdeeds I have done. Help me to face to my responsibilities and take the consequences of my actions. Amen.

PRAYER OF A NEW CITIZEN

Here I am, dear Lord, in a new country called the U.S. It is a beautiful place. I like it a lot but, Lord, I find myself in a terrible situation. Lord, I know you said not to worry for if you can take care of the birds and the flowers then you surely will take care of me. And so, Lord, I am putting my faith in you to deliver me. Amen.

PRAYER FOR GUIDANCE

Dear Lord, please help me and guide me during these rough times. Guide me in the right direction and help me to be accepted by everyone. I know you hear me and will guide me toward the best decision. Amen.

PRAYER FOR THE MISUNDERSTOOD

I feel so alone, but am surrounded by everyone. I am distant and scared.
I don't understand why people misunderstand me! But Lord, you are my light of understanding. Help me understand this predicament. Please help me. Amen.

PRAYER OF ONE WHO IS A LEADER

God, give me knowledge to know what's right, strength to carry out these duties, patience to handle the problems that occur, and judgement to decide when to speak and when to listen. Help me to lead as your Son led, that is, by example. We ask this through Christ who leads us all. Amen.

FAILURE

Dear God, please help me to think better of myself. Please make me see that I am not a failure but a worthwhile person who believes in myself. Please make things around me better. Help me and other people around the world to find the greatest love of all, You. Amen.

PRAYER ABOUT TALENTS

Dear Lord, help me to bring out my talents through practice, prayer, and your help. Lord, help me to belong. I implore you to help. I know your love will come through for me and everyone. Amen.

WHEN I AM FEELING BLUE

Lord, how I wish things were better.
Then I wouldn't write this letter.
I would only have to say
I'm having a real great day.
I would not feel so sad
If my day weren't so bad.
I'd be treated like a queen
In my new designer jeans.
When I really do feel blue
I'll try to think of you.
A day filled up with sun
Would be forever fun.
Lord, I wish things were better.
Amen.

ON GIVING UP ON MYSELF

Lord, I was so good but now I'm bad. It really makes me feel sad. No one believes how good I was. I feel like giving up because I keep on sliding down and I feel like a clown. Dear God, don't give up on me. Give me your overflowing cup of love. May there be peace in me like a dove. Amen.

PRAYER OF AN ADDICT

Lord, I have become addicted to your creation. It gives me a high and I can't get myself out of this trap. Lord, I need your help to give me strength. Let me be free from this weed and let me grow freely once again. Amen.

PRAYER FOR STRENGTH

Lord, times are not always easy and sometimes the road can get rough. In times like this it is easy to forget that you are there for me and that there are people who care. Please, Jesus grant me the strength to go on and make the right decisions. Help me to remember you are there to lean on and to guide me. Lord, let me persevere and live the life you would be proud of. I am weak and I am not always able to resist temptation. Help me Lord, give me that strength and stand by me. Help me to see the light of your ways so that I may do the right thing. Amen.

PRAYER OF A NEW NEIGHBOR

Lord, help me to understand this new environment. Help me to understand why people don't like me just because I'm different. Help these people to understand me; to accept me and accept my ways of doing things differently. I realize I am different but that can bring us together also. Amen.

+

I AM A PERSON, NOT A PUPPET

Dear Lord, even though it makes me unlike the others, I need your help so that I won't be used. I want to be my own person. I want to be your person. Help me, O God, to be true to my ideals and true to you. Amen.

PRAYER OF ONE WHO WANTS DESIGNER JEANS

Dear Lord, I come to you with a problem, and I know you can solve it. You said in the Bible, "Cast all your burdens upon me and they shall be forgiven." Lord, in the name of Jesus I come to you with this problem. All my friends have nice clothes and designer jeans and my Mom and Dad don't have enough money to buy me these types of clothes and designer jeans.

Lord, I know there must be a way. Maybe you can help my parents get a new job; a bigger and better job, so not only I will have things but my family will have them as well.

Lord, I am not asking you out of selfishness. You said that I shall prosper, and you said ask and I shall give. Lord, this is from the heart and not of flesh—if

it is take this feeling away. Lord, I please
ask you out of faith—can I afford to have
the kind of clothes that my friends have
and the designer jeans as well? *If it is
your will, Lord!* In the name of Jesus,
I ask you. Amen.

ASKING GOD'S HELP IN TIME OF TROUBLE

Dear God, in times of strife and sorrow,
please give us the strength and courage
to follow your example. In our world
today, it is very hard to always choose
the right direction in which to follow.
Help us to see your light and live our
lives the way you did. Amen.

PRAYER WHEN I AM AFRAID

I am afraid, dear Lord, so help me.
Shine your light upon my darkness.
Show me the way and I shall walk. For I
know you will lessen my burdens.
Amen.

FAILURE

Lord, it's so hard to disregard. It's one
of the hardest to ignore. Yet, it can
happen to anyone. I pray, God, to help
me not to go alone so deep in life. I want
to succeed. Help me so that I may
disregard and ignore failure. Amen.

I WISH THINGS WERE BETTER

Dear God, I wish things were not the way they are. You don't want them this way. I wish I could wake up one morning and know that the day will bring me pleasure. Help me, God, that better things will come my way so I can look forward to the new day from now on. Amen.

✝

FAILURE

God, no matter how hard I try, I don't always succeed. I know that failure is a fact of life, but I find it difficult to deal with. Please help me to succeed a little more often. Thank you. Amen.

PRAYER OF ONE WHO FAILED A TEST

I may not have tried my best, dear God, on this test but I know that I, too, must contribute if I am to pass. For the next time, please give me the wisdom to study and not to depend on you for all of the test. I promise to try my best and to use all the good abilities you have given me. Amen.

PRAYER OF A STRANGER

Here I am today, in a strange country with people unknown; in cities unheard of; seaching for life. I feel rejected, and tired. I feel that way everywhere I turn; everywhere I go. All paths lead to disappointment. Give me the love that everyone deprives me of. With your guidance, I will make it in this country so different from my own. I have faith in you, Lord. Amen.

PRAYER OF A GIRL WHO WISHES SHE WERE PRETTY

Dear God, I don't know who to talk to or where to go for advice. Kids in school tease me all the time about how I look. Everyone's pretty except me. What should I do? Well, I guess if you follow God I know you will help me. Maybe looking pretty really doesn't count when you have God. Help us all to be kind to others and to respect others. Why are people so cruel? Do they really mean what they say? Thank you. Amen.

✛

PRAYER OF ONE WHO IS MOVING

We are moving, Lord. Give me courage and strength to leave my friends and start again. I want to be accepted by my new community. Thank you for all the happiness you have given me and please continue to help me. Amen.

PRAYER OF ONE WHO IS SICK

Dear God, please help me. I am very sick and can't lead a normal life. All my friends go out and have fun while I sit home lying in my bed. I am afraid I will get worse. I am asking to feel better and be able to live my life. I want to be able to do all the things the other kids do. While I lie in bed I think of everything that can happen to me. I'm afraid. Help me to understand. Why does it have to be me? I am so young and have so much to look forward to. Life can be so unfair. I love you God. Do you love me? Amen.

PRAYER OF A FRESHMAN

Dear Lord, I am starting my first year of high school. I don't know anyone here and I am really scared. Lord, I don't know how to act. I'm afraid that if I act like myself they may not accept me. I feel as if anything I say or do is wrong. So Lord, I am asking for your guidance in showing me what to do and say to help me get through the rest of the year with a few friends. Thanks for listening to me. I am not expecting miracles but know you will answer my prayers. Amen.

PRAYER OF ONE WHO IS SUFFERING

Dear Lord,
Why is my life full of sorrow?
Why am I booed and shunned?
Why can't my life be any other?
Full of laughter and fun?
Lord,
Was I meant to suffer?
To feel the hurt and pain
Of all the teasing?
Their friendship never to gain?
What did I do to deserve this?
Where did I go wrong?
If I did, Lord, I pray to you now
That I will just belong. Amen.

✝

PRAYER OF A NEW CITIZEN

Dear Father, please help the people around me in this new land understand the trouble I'm going through. Urge them to help me instead of ridiculing me. I have no friends, no money, no food, no home. I am alone and scared. Assist me to get through these hard times I am going through. Also assist these people to understand and even help me to pass through this rough period in my life. Amen.

✝

PRAYER OF ONE WHO HAS LOST A GAME

Jesus, when we lose a game or lose our matches or anything else, we hope you can give us the strength to be good sports. Give us strength to congratulate our opponents for winning. Give us the strength to try harder next time out. Amen.

PRAYER FOR BELONGING

God, I need someplace
To call home.
Some place warm in winter
And cool
In summer.
It has to have a window
So I can look
Upon the beautiful
Things you have created.
And it has to have
A door that I may
Welcome a stranger.
It has to have running
Water so that I may
Cleanse my body.
And it has to have someone who loves
Me to abide with me.
Until you can find me
This place, I will
Live here, in the
Center of your
HEART. Amen.

IT'S GOOD TO BE ALIVE

When I smell the flowers
When I hear the birds sing,
I know it's good to be alive.
When someone says, ''I love you,''
When I know someone's there to care
I know it's good to be alive.
When things go wrong and they always
	will
I know they will get better and
When they do I say to myself ''It's good
	to be alive.''
Amen.

✝

IT IS GOOD TO BE ALIVE

It's good to wake up in the morning to see the sun shine; to hear the birds sing; to see the first signs of spring. To hear people laughing, singing your praise... this makes me want to face the long days. The laughter of children playing with friends makes you pray the world won't end. It's good to be alive; to hear; to see; to love and treasure the things you have given me, God. Amen.

PRAYER OF A NEW CITIZEN

Father, I understand that I may be new to this country but I don't understand why people have to treat me like I am inhuman or abnormal. I do have a bit of a problem trying to adjust to this kind of life and environment, but I pray to you so you can help me get myself together. Help people understand my problems and realize that they could be in my predicament one day. I believe you can help. Amen.

+

PRINTED IN BELGIUM BY

proost

INTERNATIONAL BOOK PRODUCTION